"AND THE SONS OF PULLMAN PORTERS
AND THE SONS OF ENGINEERS
RIDE THEIR FATHERS' MAGIC CARPETS
MADE OF STEEL."

FROM *THE CITY OF NEW ORLEANS*
SUNG BY ARLO GUTHRIE
WRITTEN BY STEVE GOODMAN

⊶ DEDICATION ⊷
THIS BOOK IS DEDICATED TO THE DESCENDANTS
OF OUR PULLMAN PORTERS.

⊶ ACKNOWLEDGMENTS ⊷

MIKE BLANC

SHEILA TARR

KRISTIN BLACKWOOD

JENNIE LEVY SMITH

KURT LANDEFELD

CAROL LANDEFELD

SONYA VICK FISHCO

A. VAN JORDAN

DANIEL TOBIN

THE PULLMAN PORTER

VanitaBooks, LLC All rights reserved.
Copyright ©2014 Vanita Oelschlager.

⊶ ADDITIONAL COPYRIGHTS ⊷
The City of New Orleans ©1971 Steve Goodman, Rising from the Rails ©2004 Larry Tye
A Long Hard Journey, The Story of the Pullman Porter ©1989 Patricia and Fredrick McKissack.

Hardcover Edition ISBN: № 978-1-938164-00-2   Paperback Edition ISBN: № 978-1-938164-01-9

Text by Vanita Oelschlager   Design and illustration by Mike Blanc   Printed in the USA

⊶ WWW.VANITABOOKS.COM ⊷

The PULLMAN PORTER

an American Journey

⚬⊷ WRITTEN BY ⊶⚬

VANITA OELSCHLAGER

with

⚬⊷ ART BY ⊶⚬

MIKE BLANC

VanitaBooks, LLC

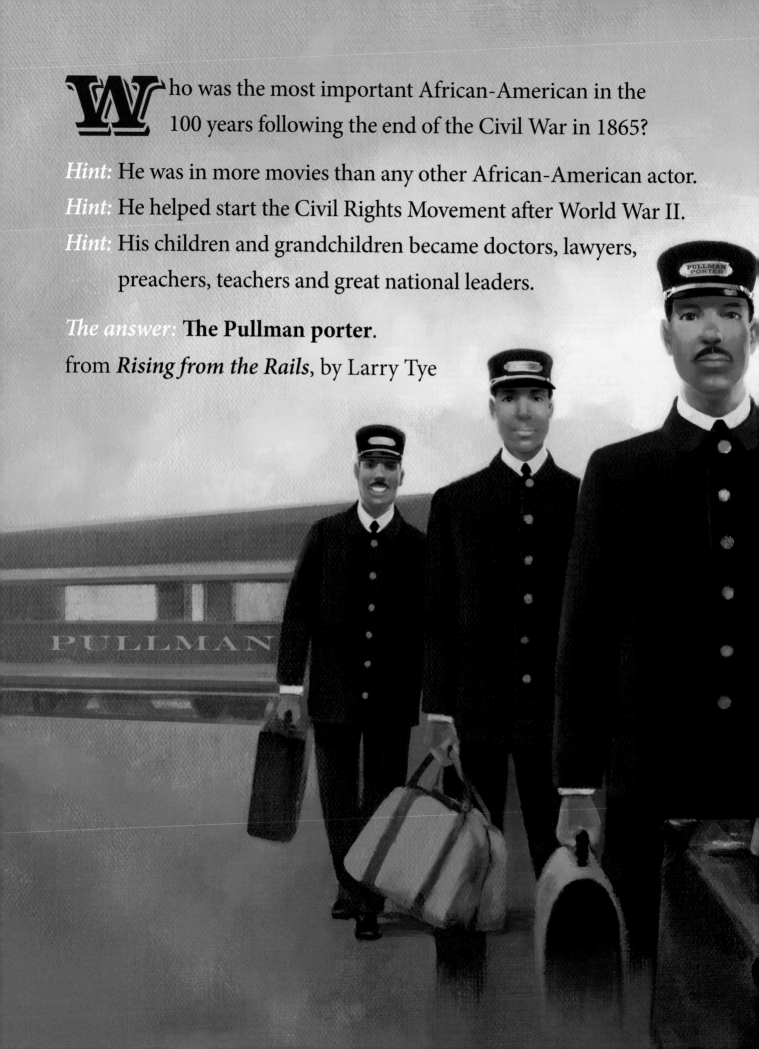

Who was the most important African-American in the 100 years following the end of the Civil War in 1865?

Hint: He was in more movies than any other African-American actor.

Hint: He helped start the Civil Rights Movement after World War II.

Hint: His children and grandchildren became doctors, lawyers, preachers, teachers and great national leaders.

The answer: **The Pullman porter.**

from *Rising from the Rails*, by Larry Tye

Railroad trains were in use in the United States by the 1830s. By the end of the Civil War trains were carrying Americans from Boston and New York west to Chicago and St. Louis, and south to Denver, San Francisco and Seattle.

Travel was very uncomfortable. The trip was dirty and noisy. You had to sleep in your seat or on a hard bunk bed stacked along the train wall. If you wanted to eat along the way, you had to bring your own food.

A man from Chicago, George Pullman, saw an opportunity. He built the first fancy sleeping and dining railroad cars. He knew that wealthy travelers would pay more money to be served fine meals and sleep in beds with real mattresses and fine linens. The cars were warmed by an in-floor furnace and lit with candles. The Pullman Sleeping Car was invented in 1857.

After the Civil War freed the slaves, George Pullman hired the best and brightest ex-slaves to work in his Pullman train cars as porters. They had just been freed and needed jobs to provide for their families.

Working on a train seemed like a wonderful way to see

the country. The ex-slaves got good jobs on sleeper cars.

These jobs were considered romantic by their neighbors,

friends and family, even symbols of freedom. Porters

became the most respected members of their communities.

The jobs in reality were degrading and difficult.

Station porters carried luggage for passengers and supplies for the train.

The porter was part maid, shoeshine boy, nurse and calmer of temper tantrums. He was the first person to greet passengers as they entered the station and the last to see them on their way at the end of the trip.

Porters carried a rule booklet in their pocket at all times. There were very specific ways a porter was to deal with situations as they arose. Here are two rules:

"To get rid of a fly you need to darken the cabin and then leave one window open in the rear for the fly to escape."

"To wake a passenger you were not to open his curtain, but to gently shake it and whisper the passenger's name."

Sometimes, against the rules, the porter tossed food to hungry children as the train whisked by.

The main task of the porters was to make the beds at night and turn them back into seats in the morning. The Pullman porter pulled down the beds and made them in three to five minutes. He made the beds when the passengers headed to the dining car for supper. If the bed wasn't made right the passenger might fall out of bed at night.

The porter even cared for newborns and toddlers, sometimes in a separate car. Pullman maids sometimes held this job. Pullman porters catered to all the needs of the male as well as the female passengers.

Most porters were between 5' 7" to 6' 1" in height. They were usually not younger than 25 or older than 40, but many of them lied about their ages to get jobs.

The appearance of the Pullman porter had to be perfect. His fingernails were clean, his mustache was trimmed and he wore a white coat to make the beds. He wore a black cap and blue jacket for greeting passengers and carrying their bags. Pullman porters had to provide their own shoe polish to shine people's shoes. They also had to buy their own uniforms and hats.

A porter was often gone for long periods of time.
Sometimes his family would not see him for weeks.

Porters worked in pairs. Each pair took care of two cars.
At night, one porter had to be awake at all times. They slept
in four-hour shifts. Their bed was a thin cushion covering
a cramped couch in the smoking room. It was a hard way
to work and sleep.

The porter wasn't paid much by the hour. He relied on tips for much of his income. He earned tips by doing extra things for passengers like shining shoes and caring for their children.

It was said that Sarah Heinz, wife of H.J. Heinz the ketchup maker, was the best tipper of all.

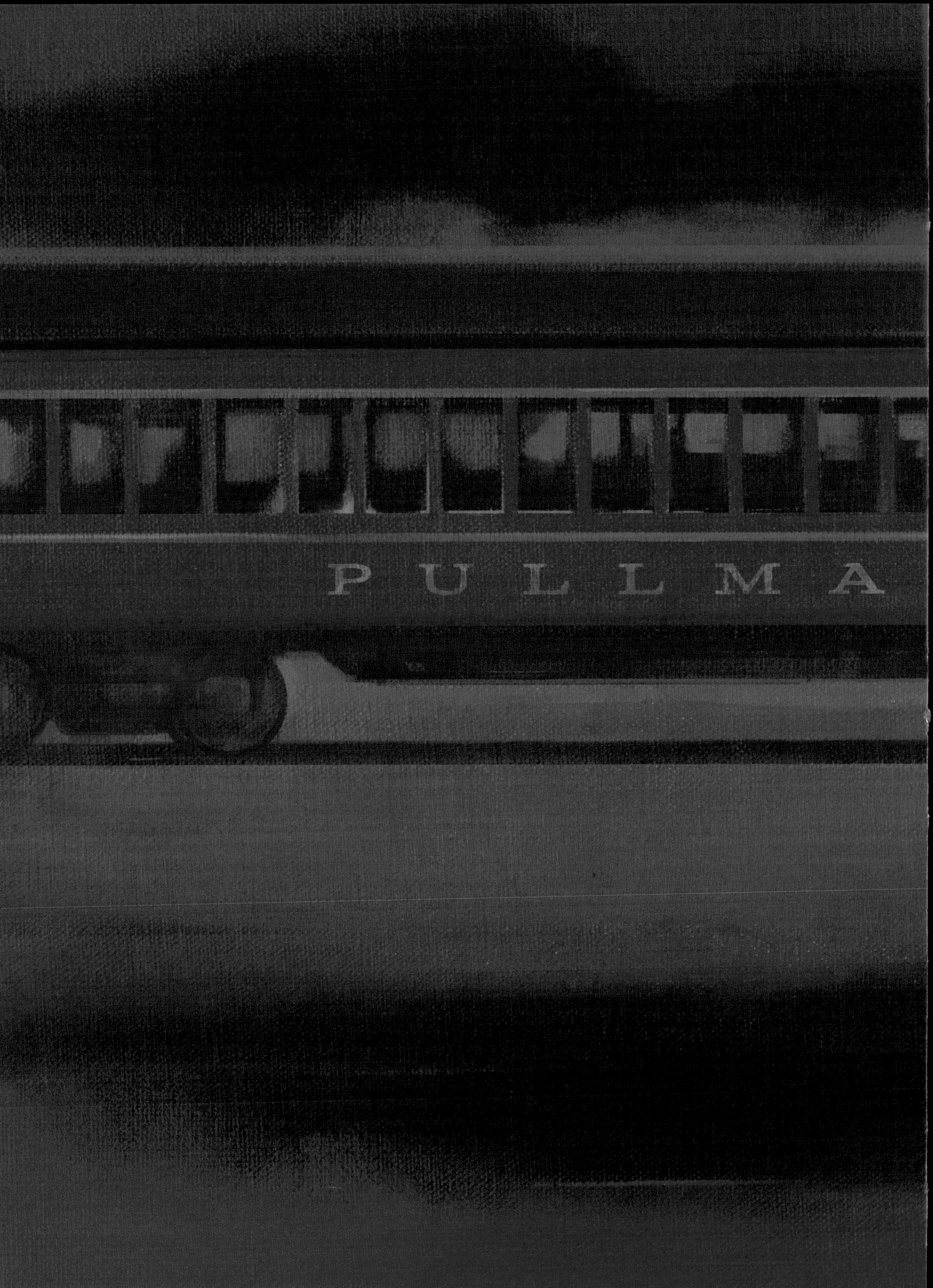
PULLMA

Passengers often did not care to learn the names of the porters in their cars. So they would call them "George" instead, after George Pullman. This was embarrassing to a porter but he had to accept it to keep his job and earn tips.

Education was an important part of strengthening African-American families for the equal rights struggle ahead.

The porter would look, listen and learn from the passengers. He would read the papers they left behind, listen to them talk to one another and learn all he could.

The porter learned how important education was for children and took this message home to his children.

By the 1920s the Pullman porters had become a fixture on American trains. They worked 240 hours a month and sometimes only got $10 for it. In 1925, with the help of a very brave African-American, A. Philip Randolph, they began to form a union for better pay and working conditions.

But it wasn't until 1937 that Randolph and the porters finally got their union and were able to get better wages and working conditions from George Pullman's company. It was called the *Brotherhood of Sleeping Car Porters*.

President Franklin D. Roosevelt and his wife, First Lady Eleanor Roosevelt helped The Brotherhood. They would listen to them and set up meetings for them to meet with other unions.

Abraham Lincoln's son, Robert Todd Lincoln ran the Pullman Company

after George Pullman died. He was helpful to The Brotherhood also.

He was more pleasant to meet with than George Pullman had been.

The Pullman porters, headed by A. Philip Randolph, really can be credited with starting the Civil Rights Movement. In 1956 there was the Montgomery Bus Boycott. A Pullman porter, E.D. Nixon, is credited with asking Rosa Parks to be the person who would refuse to move to the back of the bus with other African-Americans.

Soon after this, they wanted to march to Washington, D.C. to show that they wanted all the same rights as the white people. They needed a great leader. They visited church after church to find someone to lead them. When they visited Martin Luther King, Jr.'s church, he agreed to lead their march for equal rights for all people. On August 28, 1963, more than 200,000 people gathered between the Lincoln Memorial and the Washington Monument. Rich and poor came. Black and white came. Jews and Christians came. They sang *We Shall Overcome,* a labor song from the 1930s. A. Philip Randolph introduced Martin Luther King, Jr., who had insisted on a nonviolent civil protest. King gave his speech that started like this: "I have a dream, that my four little children will one day live in a nation where they will not be judged by the color of their skin but by the content of their character." That day in 1963, A. Philip Randolph handed the reins over to Martin Luther King, Jr.

Dr. Martin Luther King, Jr.

By the late 1960s Americans preferred air travel to riding on trains. The century of service the porters had done for millions of Americans was coming to an end. Pullman porters had helped lead African-Americans out of slavery. Because of their hard work, their children, grandchildren and great grandchildren were able to get better jobs, pursue an education and become part of the American dream.

"In 1969, man walked on the moon, A. Philip Randolph turned 80, and the Pullman Company stopped making rail cars. The trains went the way of the dinosaur. Airlines were the new way to travel. Pullman sleepers are now in museums."

from ***A Long Hard Journey***, *The Story of the Pullman Porter* by Patricia and Fredrick McKissack

This book was written to help us remember the Pullman porters and how important they were in our history. We owe them a large debt of gratitude because they helped make it possible for Americans to explore and settle the United States.

The Pullman porters are now part of history that has passed. It is good to remember them for their courageous struggle for equal rights and because some of the most famous African-Americans were the children or grandchildren of these great Americans.

MORE ON THE
PULLMAN PORTERS

❯ FAMOUS DESCENDANTS ❮

WHOOPI GOLDBERG
Actor/comedian: Her grandfather was a Pullman porter.

MALCOLM LITTLE AKA MALCOLM X
Courageous advocate for African-Americans' right to self-determination.

THURGOOD MARSHALL
Supreme Court Justice. He and his father were both Pullman porters.

E.D. NIXON
A Pullman porter with a sixth grade education, helped during the MONTGOMERY BUS BOYCOTT and organized a state branch of the BROTHERHOOD OF SLEEPING CAR PORTERS.

❯ LISTEN ❮

The City of New Orleans, sung by ARLO GUTHRIE, written by STEVE GOODMAN

We Shall Overcome, sung at the 1963 MARCH ON WASHINGTON

❯ READ ❮

A Long Hard Journey, *The Story of the Pullman Porter*, by PATRICIA AND FREDRICK MCKISSACK

Our Luxurious Overnight Trip, *A Family Memoir* by SONYA VICK FISHCO

Links to the listed resources may be accessed at www.VanitaBooks.com.

VANITA OELSCHLAGER <small>AND</small> MIKE BLANC

VANITA is a wife, mother, grandmother, philanthropist, former teacher, current caregiver, author and poet. She is a graduate of the University of Mount Union in Alliance, Ohio, where she currently serves as a Trustee. Vanita is also Writer in Residence for the Literacy Program at The University of Akron. She and her husband Jim received a *Lifetime Achievement Award* from the National Multiple Sclerosis Society in 2006. She won the Congressional *Angels in Adoption*™ Award for the State of Ohio in 2007 and was named *National Volunteer of the Year* by the MS society in 2008. She was honored as 2009 *Woman Philanthropist of the Year* by the United Way of Summit County. In May 2011, Vanita received an honorary Doctor of Humane Letters from the University of Mount Union. In 2013, Vanita joined The LeBron James Family Foundation to serve on its Advisory Board.

MIKE'S 35 years in graphic arts includes the illustration of countless publications for corporate and public interests worldwide. His technique includes digital illustration as well as traditional drawing and painting. Mike's work with author Vanita Oelschlager includes children's book titles; *Francesca, Postcards from a War, Porcupette Finds a Family, I Came From the Water,* and *Bonyo Bonyo, The True Story of a Brave Boy from Kenya,* with Kristin Blackwood. Mike lives with his family in Doylestown, Ohio.

ABOUT THE ART

The paintings for *Pullman Porters* were created as mixed media heavy-body acrylics on canvas with digital finish. The finished paintings were assembled in book form using Adobe® InDesign™ with Adobe® Photoshop™ for color management. Display fonts include BickhamScript, CameoAntique, Columbia Titling, Copperplate Gothic, Crash Numbering, Eisenbahn, Headliner No.45, LatinWide, Mailart Rubberstamp, Past Due and Woodtype Ornaments. Minion Pro was used for body text and was designed by Robert Slimbach for Adobe™.

NET PROFITS

VanitaBooks donates all net profits to charities where "*people help people help themselves.*" Ten percent of all net profits from this book will be donated to **FRIENDS OF WRITERS**, a not-for profit 501(c)(3) organization that enriches American poetry and fiction by cultivating new and vital literary voices that reflect the entire nation. It supports the students, alumni and faculty of its partner, the Warren Wilson College MFA Program for Writers.